My Journey:

Growing Through Grief

Michael L. Mosley

My Journey: Growing Through Grief

First Edition: February 2021. Printed in the United States of America

Cover Art: Designs by Amaya

Paperback: 978-1-7364339-2-8

My Journey: Growing Through Grief

By

Michael L. Mosley

Dedication

This book is dedicated to: my father, The Late Jerry Leon Mosley, whom I love and miss dearly, my mother Sandra Glover Mosley, who has always been there for me, my wife Porscha Tamesha Mosley, for pushing me, laughing with me, and crying with me through the process. Finally, to everyone who reads this and who has lost a loved one and has to deal with the pain of grief, I pray my story will assist you in healing.

TABLE OF CONTENTS

Table of Contents

INTRODUCTION

As with any relationship, the relationship between a father and son can be good or bad and can have its ups and downs. Contrary to popular belief, I believe the relationship is important and necessary. Sons can glean so much from their fathers, and when the relationship is healthy, and I believe it is the son's desire to one day make his father proud. My relationship with my father was just like any other father-son relationship. We had our good times and good days and as I got older and as the old people say, "started smelling myself," we would butt heads. Growing up, my father was the ultimate provider. For years it was just him, my mother, and me, and he made certain that we had everything we needed. I never realized that at times we didn't have much because of him making sure that we had everything. Early in his life, he worked for a paving company, which caused him to be out on the road and stay away from home. Although I never told him, I hated it when he had to go and stay away for a week at a time and come back on the weekends. However, even though I didn't like it, I eventually got used to it because that was how he was provided for us. As time went on, I don't know if getting used to it was a good thing or a bad thing.

I realized that with my father gone so much and with me growing up that we did not do much together. I slowly became a mama's boy because I was with her the majority of the time. There were no weekend fishing trips, although he did fish from time to time. When he was home from work, he and I did not spend a lot of extra father-son time together. However, the times we did ride together were great, and so were the conversations. He was a bit of a homebody and did not go to too many places. I would enjoy our summer trips to Philadelphia; however, even there, I would want to be with my cousins who I hadn't seen. There were many times growing up; I would envy hearing friends speak on how they and their fathers did such and such or went here or there together. Why didn't I have that luxury? Although I didn't, it did not make me dislike my father, however it did make me wonder.

As the years went on and I got older, things still continued to be the same. He still provided for us so much so that it spoiled me even into adulthood. Shortly after graduating from high school, he bought my first car, which I wrecked and totaled probably six to eight months later. Nevertheless, he came to my rescue and spoke to the attorney who in turn spoke to the judge on my behalf. I probably should not say this, but I remember standing before the judge on my court date and him not even speaking to me regarding the accident. Instead we spoke about college, work and whatever else he brought up. Some might say I received a slap on the wrist however, to me it was not even a slap; more like a tap or a pat. My father knew how to work it.

As long as I was in school, I did not have to work because he said he would take care of everything. I'm not just talking about high school, but in my two years of community college, I didn't have to want for anything. When I look back on life now, it crippled me because I would rely on him and did not have much responsibility. You can say I became like a person with two good feet who still used crutches.

Our family is not like every other family, meaning that we are not the huggy, touchy-feely family. And now that I think about it, we never really say "I love you" to each other. The fact that we loved each other went without saying, although now I know I should have said it more. The reality is that since love is an action word, we showed our love more than saying it. I knew my father loved me by his actions, and although at times we butt heads severely, I loved him and wanted to make him proud.

As time went on, my father would tell people, "one day, my son is going to be a preacher." He would say it all the time, and my sisters would hate it. Whenever I think about it now, I can't help but to laugh. He was there through just about all of my natural and spiritual elevations. When I graduated from high school as one of only two African American male, and one of ten African American honor graduates, he was there. When I graduated with my Associate's Degree, he was there with his head held high. When I was ordained a deacon, again, he was there with his head held high. As a matter of fact, I can remember the preacher at my ordination telling my father that I was fulfilling the call that was designed for him. My God! He told him that he was the cup, and I was the saucer, and he was supposed to be a deacon, but because he didn't, the contents from his cup fell onto me. At my wedding, he marched down that aisle with his chest poked out! When I preached my initial sermon (which he prophesied years earlier, telling everyone one day I would be a preacher), he was again there sitting on that front row proud. When I was ordained and installed as an Assistant Pastor, I could again see the joy in his face. I was installed as Pastor in April 2014, and he was there sitting right behind me, and you could not tell him anything. After the service, he strutted around the church as if he was the Pastor. Through all the ups and downs, the joys and hurts, the good and the bad; I made him proud.

However, later on in the year, he became sick with stage 4 colon cancer, and we did not realize before it was too late. How did I miss that something was wrong? I remember attending a funeral service some months before he was diagnosed and heard someone say to him, "you're losing weight there, aren't you?" Yet still, nothing clicked in his mind nor mine that he might be sick. My mother would constantly have to hem his uniforms because he was getting smaller. I thought that it was because of the nature of his work. They would typically have to do lots of walking so he was getting exercise. I watched him grow weak, and at times I felt helpless. While he was in the hospital, he gave my siblings and me instructions for life after he was gone. I didn't want to hear that I wanted more time. There were things that we had not talked about or done. When he came home under hospice care, I could not bear the pain of seeing him in his condition. What crushed me the most was when I came one afternoon to my parent's house to see my father. As he laid in the bedroom with my mother standing by his bedside, he looked at me and then looked up at my mother. My mother then said, "There is Michael. Do you know who he is?" My father then looked at me and then looked back at my mother and shook his head no. Afterwards, he waved at me and at that point I literally could not take it and I had to go outside. Here I was, his firstborn and only son and now he does not know who I am. Although I knew it was the disease, that still did not make it any easier. People were coming in and out of the house to see him, and it made me sick. Yes, I put on a good front, but if you weren't family, I really didn't want you coming. Then here comes the "SUPER SAINTS" trying to preach and me wanting to tell them I don't need you to tell me to hold God's unchanging hand.

Ma'am and sir, I don't need you to tell me what I know. Others came spouting off scripture only to have me wanting to tell them, "you just took that entire verse out of context." Needless to say, I did not get the time back with him that I wanted, and exactly one month to the day after my spiritual father, the late Bishop Robert Patton, had died, here we were burying my natural father. At that moment, it felt as if a great part of me had died and been buried with him. Now here we were; no more conversations, no more advice, no more laughs, no more loans, and no more food. Yes, my dad could COOK! What was I going to do now? How was life going to be now? Never in a million years would I have seen this coming. It was as if a professional boxer had hit me with a body shot, knocking the wind out of me. My mind flashed back to when I was a child, and he would leave to go to work for that paving company, but only this time, he would not return.

We all deal with grief differently, and while everyone gave me props for how strong I stood to deliver his eulogy (which was only by the grace of God), the fact is on the inside, I was hurting and a mess. This was life-altering and something that I could not control. Who would have known after he died the changes that I would find myself in the days to come? Listen, no matter how strong we think we are in our own eyes or in the eyes of others, life has a way of breaking you down the least common denominator. At this point in my life, I was broken. Now, I want to take you into my part of my life and give you a transparent look at my own internal struggles and how I almost allowed grief to transform me into a different person! I want to take you into my process and allow you to see that no matter how saved we are, we are still human. My prayer is that my story will help you if and when you find yourself in a similar situation. Come on in, and let's read!

MENTAL

My Journey: Growing Through Grief

The brain is responsible for sending signals to the rest of the body. Grief has a way of interrupting the normal functioning of the brain in that it affects the limbic system. The limbic system is a complex system of nerves and networks in the brain, involving several areas near the edge of the cortex concerned with instinct and mood. It controls the basic emotions (fear, pleasure, anger) and drives (hunger, sex, dominance, care of offspring). This limbic system controls some behaviors that are essential to everyday life. Grief can throw off how we regulate our emotions, our ability to multi-task, our ability to concentrate, and our memory. The pain of loss can be so overwhelming that you feel all types of emotions. In a nutshell, this was what was happening to me.

I had no clue as to what was happening in my life in the days and weeks after my father died. Why was I feeling off? Why couldn't I remember what seemed to be simple things, such as passwords, and why would I repeatedly tell my wife things that I had just told her the day before. I now know that it was the grief that had affected my limbic system. There were things at work that my supervisor asked me to do that I would forget and because I am that individual that will take things to the extreme, I began researching dementia. Don't judge me. Some of you are like that too! I never told anyone before, but there was a time where I was coming home from work, and I literally forgot where I was going. So you can understand why I researched dementia, right? I thought I was losing my mind.

The moment my father died, I did not cry. There was a pain and then a numbness that came over my body like a dentist giving a shot of Novocain. I literally thought something was wrong with me. Yes, I loved my father dearly, and today I would give anything to have him back, but at that moment, even when I tried to cry, I just could not. However, what I wish was that someone would have told me that grief can take time to settle in. What I was experiencing is called delayed grief, and it is just as it sounds. Delayed grief is grief that you do not fully experience until sometime after your loss. This delay can happen anywhere from weeks to months after the death and funeral. The shock that came from losing my father made me hold off on grieving so that I could help my family, who was grieving and work through getting things together for his funeral. Although I am sometimes heralded as the strong one in the family because I am a Pastor, the reality was that immediate grieving for me at this time was too overwhelming to cope with. Therefore, I just bottled it all up inside and suppressed it, which resulted in other issues.

Once the delayed grief finally hit me, it was just as if I was experiencing immediate grief. I can recall being in Charlottesville, Virginia, on my way to work when all of a sudden, there it was. It was like a Mack truck sideswiping a car in an intersection or maybe more like a tsunami sweeping over a small village; the sadness was devastating and almost unbearable. It was totally out of the blue. I began to yell and cry uncontrollably. I made it to the Food Lion parking lot on Avon Extended, and I sat there and beat the steering wheel of my car while tears and snot flooded my face all the way down to the seat of my car. I remember feeling a storm of emotions: sadness, anger, guilt, and just a raw gut-wrenching hurt. Then the memories started flooding my mind. I was thinking about the times that I hurt my father because I knew how to hurt him and what hurt him. All the times that I wouldn't talk to him which would make him so upset began to flood my mind and I wanted to apologize all over again. I was thinking about the times that I made him upset or the times that I disappointed him. I just felt the guilt and shame of all the things that I did. Things which I apologized for, but nevertheless they were done. My mind went back to how even in all that he would still give me his last if he had it, he would still come and fix anything that was broken in my home or still come cut our grass if it needed. I sat and sat and sat with these emotions, and I cried and cried and cried some more. I know people probably thought I was crazy; however, at that moment, there was no one but me and this grief that now decided rear its head.

Once I somewhat got myself together, I realized that I was going to be late to work, AGAIN, so this is what I did. Are you ready? I went into Food Lion and bought Visine Advanced Relief, a tube of petroleum jelly, and came back out to my car and put on my mask. Not a literal mask, but the pretentious face that I was alright. After soaking my eyes with Visine Advanced (which, by the way, worked wonders), and putting Vaseline on my face to cover the tears, I began to practice my fake smile. Ok, listen, I'm not only helping me, but I'm trying to help you too. I literally sat there and smiled in the mirror because I knew that once I got to work, people were going to ask me how was I doing, and God forbid I say that I am horrible, jacked-up, hurt, angry, and tired; no, I had to keep up appearances and the picture of everything be great in spite of. Hear me, that is hard to do when day in and day out you have something tearing at you inside.

If that wasn't enough, I began to let fear grip me. I can hear you asking, fear of what? The short answer is dying or death. In medical terms, it is called Thanatophobia. Thanatophobia is simply the fear of death. I watched my father die of colon and liver cancer, and not just in the back of my mind, but all over my mind, I began to think, I am going to die of this too. Now, did I have the actual full phobia? I don't believe so, but what I did have was what I believe was an extension of it from the grief affecting the limbic system. I got to the point in which every ache and pain I felt I began to think it was cancer. I would literally lose sleep some nights and would be up and down and back and forth. I would think to myself in the middle of the night, when is this cycle going to end. I want to be able to lay down and get a good night's sleep and not feel like when I closed my eyes that I was not going to wake up the next morning.

My mind was literally spinning like a child pumping a spinning top. I had to tell myself repeatedly; you're not going to die. However, the thought of my wife being without a husband and my children being without a father overwhelmed to the point where it happened. Now you're probably asking yourself what IT is. Well, here is what IT is. After another restless night of sleep, I am once again up and on my way to work. I make it on to Avon Street Extended in Charlottesville, Virginia, when all of a sudden, I feel my heart starting to race, accompanied by pains in my chest. In my mind, I thought I was having a heart attack, and this was going to be it. I did everything in my power to try to breathe as I felt myself having shortness of breath accompanied by heavy sweating. I found a place to pull over and sit and try to calm myself while tears rolled down my face like a flood. I felt like I was going to die. However, after a few moments, things began to subside, but that feeling scared me even more. I realized that I had just had a panic or anxiety attack. I don't know if they are different or one and the same; however, I don't think I would wish that on my worst enemy. There have been times when people would tell me about these, and my response would be for them to just suck it up, however now I know because I have had the experience. However, that did not stop me from thinking about when I was going to have another one.

As time went on, I felt as if I was becoming out of touch with reality. I mean, my life and daily routine were one of just going through the motions. To sum it all up, I was just sad. I know what you are thinking; you are saying Michael, you were depressed. Alright, as hard as I did not want to admit it, I was depressed. However, I would never say it out of my mouth. After all, that's what we do in the black community, right? We don't ascribe to depression, although more people now today are beginning to speak more on it. Instead, we just have moments of sadness, and then we get over it. But why does it feel like this isn't going anywhere if we just get over it? I had all of the symptoms of depression: trouble concentrating, trouble remembering details, trouble making decisions, overeating, insomnia, fatigue, irritability, restlessness, pessimism, feelings of guilt, and even suicidal thoughts and some actions. I know that I should have sought therapy; however, that was another stigma in the black community that, for some time, I believed in. We do not go to therapists or counselors. Instead, we man up and deal with it and get over it. However, getting over it was better said than done.

The depression was causing me to spiral mentally until I started having suicidal thoughts. Yes, me Michael Mosley, with my tongue talking, worshipping, laying hands, praying Heaven down self was having suicidal thoughts. I found myself at times telling myself that my wife and daughters would be better off without me, and at least they would have good money if I just ended it all. I found myself asking my daughters what they would do if they didn't have me. There were a couple of occasions where I played Russian roulette with my life. I can recall driving to work and, on a number of occasions, closing my eyes while on curvy and winding Route 20. One such time I closed my eyes about a little way up from this bridge called Carter's Bridge, but for some odd reason, my car stayed on the road. There were a number of times where I would run red lights hoping to run head on to another car or truck and just be done with it all, but it never happened. I know what you're thinking, Michael; Why didn't you just get a knife or gun. The short answer to that is, although I have access to all of that, it was just too simple. I know it sounds crazy, but that's just how I was thinking at the time. If I was going out, it would be with a bang. Here is the thing, I don't think I necessarily wanted to kill myself (at least I don't think so), but I was looking for a way to deal with the pain because, at the moment, I was not. This was about to be a new life for my family and me, a life without my father that was unwanted, and for a while, I felt as if I didn't belong in it either.

I would often think if I would ever make it through this grief of mine, knowing that there really is no right or wrong way to do this. Somehow I had to pull my mind and thoughts together knowing that after he died in March, in 4 months we would be celebrating his birthday, in 5 months, we would celebrate our parents anniversary, in 8 months, we would have our first Thanksgiving without him, and then in 9 months, we would have our first Christmas without him, but at the same time knowing that he was diagnosed on Christmas Eve the year before. What a Christmas present. This would be tough, but I knew that I had to get it together; my family depended on me, but I would wonder who would be there for me to depend on...

PHYSICAL HEALTH

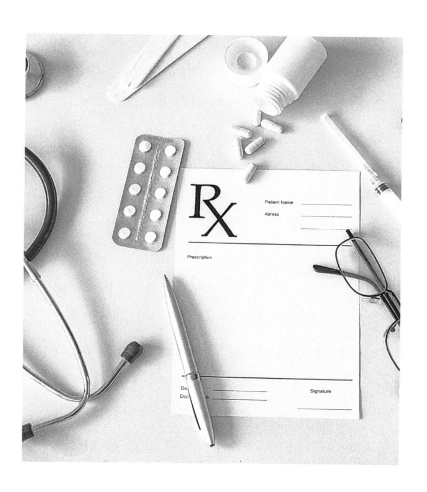

My Journey: Growing Through Grief

Traumatic events such as the death of a loved one can cause you to plunge into an abyss of inescapable and overwhelming pain. We often mistake grief as a single emotion. However, it is really multifaceted and sometimes uncontrollable. I can recall sitting at my parent's dining room table when my uncle yelled, "Jerry, Jerry; he's gone" and feeling a jolt that I cannot fully explain run throughout my body. If I remotely tried to explain what that moment felt like, it was as if a part of me left or died right then. I stood in the door looking somewhat afraid to go into the room, all while hearing the cries of my mother, sisters, and aunts. I immediately ran out and called my supervisor and the undertaker and gathered the children into the other room. However, as I attempted to console everyone, I wondered to myself, why am I not crying. What is wrong with me?

My father was gone, and not one tear from me. Grief can be similar to a wild roller coaster. At any given time, you can hit a bump or speed around a turn that you didn't know was coming.

There were a tremendous bump and turn that was about to come into my life, and I didn't see it.

My Journey: Growing Through Grief

Grief can tremendously affect our physical well-being. Well, the truth is I wanted to drink. I can recall pacing back and forth in front of a liquor store in Charlottesville, Virginia, while on my lunch break. I wanted to go in so badly and get a bottle and just drown my pain and drown my sorrow. This was dangerous for me because earlier in life, I had some issues with alcohol. However, there was still that pull from the

Holy Spirit that kept telling me, "don't do it, don't do it." You see, God is such a gentleman in that He will give you a warning, but He will never override your will. That's it, I've made up my mind, I am going in. Just when I walked back up and was about to put my hand on the door, I hear a voice say, "Hey, Reverend Mosley!" I look, and it's a lady that I know, and we begin to carry on a conversation as I played it off as if I was just walking up and down the sidewalk. God is so funny! So I guess getting drunk just was not meant to be, but there was something else that had invaded my life.

One of the most common effects of grief on a person's physical health is a loss of appetite, which in turn leads to weight loss. When you experience such a great loss, you can become too distressed to feel hungry or even remember to eat. The truth is that hunger can become a mere secondary need for your body when you already feel empty. However, for me, it was the opposite. I turned to food, and I turned HARD! There is such a thing as "comfort food." Comfort food is defined as food that provides consolation or a feeling of well-being, typically any with high sugar or other carbohydrate content. Comfort food is food that provides a nostalgic or sentimental value to someone and maybe characterized by its high caloric nature, high carbohydrate level, or just simple preparation. The nostalgia may be specific to an individual, or it may apply to a specific culture. Well, let's just say for me, food became more than just comfort. It became my addiction, my way of escape; it became my obsession.

What I found out is that overeating or emotional eating after the death of a loved one is called "grief eating." In grief, what we do is we try to find something to soothe us, and for me, food and sodas had become that something. I often found myself eating just to be eating. There were times where I know I was not hungry, but yet I would go and grab something, whether it was food or junk food. There was no slowing down! I can remember my wife even telling me one time, "Now Mike, I know you are not hungry!" I would just say yes, I am and proceed to eat as if I didn't have a care in the world. While at work, Mountain Dew had become my addiction. I was drinking fifteen per week. Yes, you read correctly, FIFTEEN! I literally had one for breakfast, one for lunch, and then another in the late afternoon. I was spiraling out of control and did not have a clue as to what was about to happen.

While at my wellness checkup with my primary care physician, I can recall him coming in and saying to me, "you've put on quite a bit of weight there." When one of the nurses took my weight, she told me, "you hide it well." I didn't look as if I weighed as much as I did because of the clothes that I wore. I had noticed the weight gain, but I didn't care. My whole response to myself was, it is what it is! However, I did notice that the food still was not totally filling the void that was missing, although it did give temporary relief. As I continued to gain weight, I can remember going to a service at a local church in our community. As I walked through the door, there was a lady who I know that came up to me, hugged me, and said, "please lose some weight, ok, please lose some weight." I looked at her eye to eye for a moment before walking off hurt. In my mind, I was saying, "can't you see!" You claim to be so spiritual but can't you look deeper and see my hurt and pain. As Smokey Robinson said, if you look closer, you can trace the tracks of my tears. The tracks were there, but no one could see them or even took time to notice. This was more than just me gaining weight, but this was me trying to fill a void and an emptiness and what was about to happen next on this roller coaster was a bump that I had never imagined.

I knew because of my eating; I have gained nearly thirty pounds in a very short time. I believe it was over a span of a few months. Well, I was at a church conference when I first noticed that my pants were not fitting the same as they used to. I really didn't say anything; I just went on. After the conference, I began to notice it again, but I would just tighten my belt and keep it moving. Then other things started happening. Other than losing weight, I was sleeping a lot, having headaches, constantly getting up in the middle of the night to use the bathroom, had dry mouth, and my vision was weird. What in the world is going on here! While at work, I would have to take my glasses off to see my computer because, with them, my vision was blurry. This was strange to me as I have to wear glasses. While on the way home from work one afternoon, I fell asleep twice behind the wheel. WHOA! I know I got over eight hours of sleep the night before, and that's when I realized that something is seriously off. I called my primary care physician and told them what was happening, and they told me to get into the office immediately. I was just there not too long ago, so what is this. The nurse called me back and asked me to step on the scale in which afterward she said, whoa, you have lost close to forty pounds since you've last been here, and that was just a few months ago. I speak with my doctor, and he tells me they are going to run a few tests. They proceeded to take my blood pressure, and it was SKY HIGH. I can't exactly remember the numbers, but they were up there. They then proceeded to draw blood to take my blood sugar, and when the nurse got the reading, her eyes nearly jumped out of their sockets. She said, "Michael, your blood sugar is 435!" I was then told that I more than likely did not fall asleep behind the wheel but passed out because of the high blood sugar and blood pressure. I was also told that I was lucky not to have a stroke or heart attack because of the blood sugar and blood pressure numbers. Well, if you haven't guessed it, then here it is! Because of how I handled my grief, I literally ate myself into high blood pressure, diabetes, and acquired a potassium deficiency.

I was a wreck! High blood pressure and diabetes, REALLY? Those who know me know that I have the tendency at times to take things to the extreme. On my own, I began to read things about diabetes and high blood pressure, and I instantly went to the parts about blindness, losing limbs, heart attacks, and strokes. Although this is serious, I am taking things to the extreme. This means that I am going to have to be on medications, and that is something that I did not want. My doctor started me off with two different types of diabetic medicines, which made me sick to my stomach, but I had to take them. My blood sugar was so high that my vision temporarily corrected itself and I did not need to wear glasses, and could see clearly without them. This was crazy. However, it put somewhat of a strain on my family. My mother and sisters were worried about me and wanted me to get it together. My wife was worried; however, she continued to encourage me and speak life to my situation, although at times, I didn't want to hear it. I wondered if anyone else knew or could see the difference in weight loss since it all came so fast. I am somewhat self-conscious and, after all, didn't want folk to think that the Pastor was on crack or some other drug. As it turns out, there were folk who noticed the weight loss but were apprehensive about approaching me with regards to it. People would say things like, "you're looking good," or they would ask if I was working out. In reality, I know they wanted to dig deeper to find out what was going on, and I know that many had made assumptions, but it never came out until later.

After the high blood pressure and diabetes came a potassium deficiency. Now, I did not acquire this until a month or so after the blood pressure and diabetes. Most people would never know or recognize that I have this, but I sure did, and I was good at playing it off. The first time I noticed this was after a night of preaching. Yes, with all that was going on, I did not take a break, even from preaching. I was preaching a revival one evening, and after I was done preaching and praying for individuals on the altar, I came back to the pulpit, sat down, and that's when it first happened. My legs began to cramp as well as my hands. I could not stand up as my wife had to hold Gatorade to my mouth to drink as my hands were cramped to the point that I could not grasp the bottle. However, I did not try to take them off of the pulpit chair. No one was aware of what was going on as they all just thought I was exhausted from ministering, and I was told to just take my time and sit as long as I needed until I regained strength. However, strength was not what I needed at the moment. It was due to potassium deficiency and honestly, what I needed was a couple of bananas. Guess what happened next. You guessed it, more medicine. Here I am, blood pressure medicine, blood sugar medicine, and now potassium medicine; this did not make things easier on my mental health. Taking all these medicines, coupled with grief, began to play with my mind.

I went down two pant sizes and could fit in clothes that I had not worn in a very long time. Although this was great and I was looking better on the outside, the truth is that the inside was far from looking better. The inside was still in pain, and not to mention the very restless and sleepless nights. My wife and my sister saw to it that I started eating better and cut down on the sodas; however, lack of rest was not helping my daily performance at work and not to mention I would cry every morning on the way to work and every afternoon on the way home. I know what you're thinking! What did I do in-between time while at work? Well, I told you earlier I wore a mask and pretended that I was ok when, in reality, I was sinking in the quicksand of emotions and not trying to escape. I eventually told some of my closest friends at work about my diabetes and high blood pressure, and I'm thankful that they were willing to hold me accountable and periodically ask about my health. I never thought that I would get to the point of being on medication. Diabetes does not run in my family; however, high blood pressure does. I was determined to be the one that would break that generational cycle and would not have it, but that was not the case. My health has been an upward fight that I am continuing to battle with today. My doctor often says to me after a visit or examination, "You are a weird case. How can you have this but still you are fine here?" It's puzzling!" Nevertheless, as puzzling as it is, I am determined to work to be off all medicines. It took a little time, but I came to the realization that I have so much to live for!

WORK

My Journey: Growing Through Grief

If there was one thing that my father modeled for us, it would have to be an excellent work ethic. He worked for a paving company for a number of years and put in over 20 plus years in the correctional center, and can you believe that in all that time at the correctional center, he never once called in sick. If he was sick, he would go to work and would possibly leave early before he would ever miss a day. He was 110% committed to the job, and it showed. He modeled to us that nothing in this life comes easy, and if you want it, then you have to work for it. I know I've adopted that type of work ethic because those on my job who know me know that Michael must really be sick if he calls out. I just don't believe in wasting days because you never know when you will need them.

However, in the back of my mind, I began to wonder, "what if never calling in sick and dealing with the stress of the job caused him to be sick?" Maybe, just maybe, the chronic stress of work contributed to the acceleration of cancer that may have been there all the time. These were the types of thoughts that crossed my mind while seeing him being honored on his deathbed for his years of service and dedication. Although, I did give them some credit for doing that, as well as setting up a memorial to my father (and allowed it to stay for some time) in the lobby of the correctional facility.

Nevertheless, I was severely affected by my own work ethic after he died. I know that I returned to work too soon. I felt I was strong enough to get back into the swing of things, or so I thought. I can recall my supervisor asking me why I was there; however, I just could not stay home. I felt as if I had to keep moving or else or else the waves of emotions would overtake me and wash me out, the same way that waves of an ocean do to a surfer. There were days while on my way to work, I literally had to pull over and cry because of pent up emotions and grief that I had yet to release. Day in and day out, I would be out of it. You could say that I was a walking zombie at work. While my body was physically behind my desk every day, my mind was not there, and neither was the ability to care. It started with me being late every day. You heard correctly, EVERY DAY! I know that some of you are wondering how late. The short answer is anywhere between thirty minutes to an hour late every day. I knew that it was wrong, and as a Pastor, I am supposed to be the example and render unto Cesar his due. However, my thoughts, or lack thereof at the time, were, "I'll be there when I get there." I know, I can hear you asking, "well, what about your supervisor?" I'll get to that in just a minute.

Did I mention that my work suffered? Well, if I didn't, here it is, my work suffered! The majority of my job deals with customer service, and during that time, I didn't want to deal with customers and sure didn't want to provide a service. It is my responsibility to process payments, mail customer membership fulfillment packets, send customers replacement cards, and to return calls and emails, among other things. Did these things always happen as they should? No! There were times that I was gravely behind on returning calls and answering emails and sat zombie-like when it came to preparing and sending out membership packets and replacement cards. Sometimes, the packets would sit on my desk or in a mail tray by my desk for days before being mailed. I would receive a number of angry calls and emails, but I did not care. I was numb to these people! They don't know me, they had no idea of what I was facing or what I was going through, and so I wanted them to be as hurt and angry as I was. I would often forget to do the simple things and make simple mistakes. There were times when I would get customer accounts mixed up or even halfway post payments that I received.

There soon became no such thing as "organization" as I would have work and paper scattered across my desk as if it was a recycling facility. Although I never let anyone know, there were days where I didn't know where anything was. Backup batches were over here, credit card payments were over there, checks were here, printed emails were there; what in the world was I doing! Here I am starting one thing and not finishing it and going on to another. Adjusting one customer's account and not completing it and having them call wondering what is happening, only for me to see that it was a couple of weeks overdue. I needed help; however, when I was asked, I would get angry.

I continued to interact with coworkers, although I gave them the representative. You know, the common fake smile and "I'm doing well" answer when in reality, I didn't want to be there. Again, I wore a mask. I didn't wish to be around many of them, and I stayed to myself. My mouth was slick with a few of them. I can remember on a couple of different occasions how a few of them came down and when they looked at my desk, I would say, "wow, you've got a lot of stuff going on there." My reply would be, "as my mother always says, if you don't want to see it, then close your eyes!" I knew there were a few who genuinely cared, but I didn't believe many of the others who say they did. Now, they very well may have, but because of my state of mind, I blocked them out and refused to accept their sympathy.

Now let me get back to my supervisor. The one thing (of many) that I can say about her is that she is extremely family-oriented. If there is something that is happening with the family, she would say, "go, don't worry about this place." She was actually one of the first people I called once my father died. I am quite sure she saw my tardiness to work, and I often wondered if that was the reason she told us that we could be in by 9:00 am. Other than the tardiness, I am certain she saw the rapid decline in my work performance during this time. Although she never said anything, I could tell she was frustrated but allowed great leeway for me, which I now immensely appreciate. I know my actions would have been disappointing to my father. Regardless of how he felt, he never let it interfere with the performance he gave at work. Now here I was, late, not caring and performing poorly. It was difficult to motivate myself to perform better, but somehow I had to. My work performance was spiraling out of control, and I didn't know what to do, where to go, or who to turn to. I did not want to appear weak or incapable of doing what I had done for over 14 plus years, but I needed help, and I wasn't quite ready to ask people or God yet.

MINISTRY

My Journey: Growing Through Grief

Ministry is not just what I do, but it is a huge part of who I am. Ministry is the giving of our time, our talents, and our treasurers to help someone else. We minister by meeting the needs of people through love and humility. Ministry includes ministering the physical, emotional, financial, mental, and vocational needs of all people, regardless of race or class. This is what I love to do and was what I was taught to do by my spiritual parents, the late Bishop Robert Patton and his wife, Evangelist Lena Patton. It was always about caring for the needs of souls and placing others before yourself. This is who I am. This is what I live and breathe for; to see men, women, and children saved, whole, healed, progressing in God, operating to their full potential, and walking out their purpose and destiny.

However, in all this, who would have known that all it would take was one event to knock me off my square. Yes, me, Michael Mosley, the preaching machine as I was called and labeled by so many. Which, by the way, I DID, AND DO NOT LIKE! No, I didn't let that go to my head because I know there are others out there who can preach circles around me, and this preaching gift and anointing came from God. Therefore, every time I minister, I make sure He receives all glory! However, after my father died, I lost something in ministry. Alright now, here we go, don't condemn me because I did that to myself, but for a moment, I lost the ability to care. Yes, you read correctly! I stopped caring for a while when it came to ministry. I can hear you asking, what did I stop caring about? Well, the short answer is EVERYTHING!

My father attended every ministry elevation that I received. On Saturday, January 8, 2005, when I was ordained as a Deacon, he was there; Saturday, March 17, 2007, when I preached my initial sermon and was licensed as a Minister, he was there; Saturday, July 18, 2009, when I was ordained and installed as an Assistant Pastor, he was there, Sunday, April 27, 2014, when I was installed as a Pastor he was there. I can remember him receiving a prophetic word at my deacon ordination, saying that "he was the cup and I was the saucer under the cup and that I was really catching and moving into every place in which he was supposed to be." He was supposed to have already been walking as a deacon, but since he wasn't, God allowed that to fall from him to me. What a powerful word!

Not only was he there for the elevations, but he was there for every anniversary and times, which I was honored in between. However, during my very first Pastoral anniversary, after the service was over and I came up to give remarks, I looked out at the congregation, and there were my mother, sisters, aunts, nieces, and nephews, but he was not there. I saw the pain in my sister's face as she cried, and it was bittersweet for me because I had eulogized him just the month before. Now here I was being honored and celebrated, but inside I really could care less. I didn't care about the accolades. I didn't care about the money, I really didn't care about any of it and would have given everything just to see him sitting beside my mother as he always did on every other occasion. After his funeral in March 2015, things shifted for me. I told you I didn't care right, well now you are about to hear it all. First, I became very upset and angry with God. Yes, you heard me, I was mad, angry, and upset to the point that I didn't care about doing the work to which I was called. People come to me all the time, asking me to pray for them for this situation and that situation. I would even hear the praise reports after I, through the power of God, had prayed for them. Guess what....I had even prayed for someone whose doctor did an x-ray and saw cancer, and they went back to the doctor, and the it was gone. I know about the healing power of God. I saw Him heal my mother from a massive stroke, and I believed that God could heal my father from stage four cancer, and I prayed for Him to do so. I mean, I labored in prayer! Day in and day out, I would be on my face before the Lord for my father. On the way to work and on the way home, I would be praying that his cancer would dry up and dissipate. I even laid hands on my father and prayed again for cancer to dry up and that he would be healed, only to watch him die! I was livid. So what better way to get back at God than to not care about doing his work with my whole heart. I know I was playing a dangerous game here because souls were at stake, and I now know that God granted me grace in this time of rebellion.

Even my prayer and study life had fallen off tremendously. I had gotten to the point where all I was doing was recycling messages to the congregation because I didn't feel like or care to seek the Lord, and I knew that they wouldn't know. Therefore, I would just look and see that I preached this one a year ago this time and would just bring it out again. Honestly, I realize I had become just like many, only going through the motions of church. I would just come in, go down the line of the program, give the Word, and then give the benediction and go home. Of course, I gave some zeal and charisma (after all, that's what they wanted right); however, it was not from a place of sincerity but rather from a place of emptiness, brokenness, and pain. Here I was not listening to God, not heeding the convictions of the Holy Spirit, and again with my church mask on ready to perform.

I did not take a break, which was a huge mistake, and I would not recommend that to anyone, no matter how long you have been saved. I went ahead preaching and evangelizing with all of this hurt, anger, and emptiness on the inside. As I said, I was pastoring then, and I know what many would think or say, "why didn't your church recommend that you take time off?" I know what I am about to say may anger some, but it is the truth. What I have learned in this walk of ministry is that sometimes (not all the time) people (not all people) could give two cents about you as long as their needs are being met. I was broken, hurting, and felt empty, but some people did not care. I can hear you asking, "well, why didn't I stop myself?" It was just like work at my secular place of employment, I felt as if I had to keep going. However, my mind was so cloudy that I didn't realize that I was doing more harm than help. Yes, God still used me in the midst of this all, but I believe that it would have been at a greater capacity if I would have just taken time.

I came to realize that I was also bleeding on the people. You see, if you never heal from hurt or what hurt you, you will bleed on people who did not cut you. Pain and death are parts of life that everyone will experience; however, it is how you deal or cope with these experiences that matter. I found myself lashing out and becoming short with people at work and especially people in the church. The truth is that in my pain and my moments of not caring, I saw this as an opportunity. I know you want to know what this was an opportunity for. Well, I had been through some things with the church folk, so I used this as an opportunity to tell people off and be slick at the mouth with people. Yes, in church! Come on now, I know some of you have been there, done that! I know that wasn't right, but I thought, well, people won't see it like that, they will just attribute this attitude to my grief. That's how I was able to mask it, just blame it on the grief!

Everything in me wanted to quit. I am not talking about just taking a break or taking a sabbatical, but I got to the point where I wanted to just step down and quit everything. I did not want to preach anymore. I did not want people to call me to pray for them. I did not feel like serving anyone; my Bible collected dust as did my prayer life. But why didn't I quit? I really don't know. Something deep on the inside just would not allow me to do it. I mean day in and day out, week in and week out, I just wanted to say "the heck (well not the heck but you get it) with it all" and not go another day doing this, but with all of the "I don't care" that had overtaken me, there was still that small percentage, that inkling of I do care lurking somewhere in me. As hard as I tried to suppress caring, and let me tell you, I truly tried, I just could not. You see when it's in you, it's in you. It was imparted in me by my spiritual parents and I could not get away from it. Later I realized that it was not that I did not care, I was just allowing the pain to speak for me.

Then one evening it just clicked, and it all hit me like a ton of bricks. Maybe you don't do it, but sometimes I will go into my bathroom, look myself in the mirror and talk to me! It is during those times that I am brutally honest with me! I remember telling myself, Michael, you need to get yourself together and do it soon! Honestly, what I really needed to do was talk to a therapist or someone trustworthy, but I didn't. I knew this journey uphill would not be easy because I had shut everyone out and suppressed my emotions, but I also knew that ministry is a part of my life and who I am. I had to make a decision on whether or not I was going to give God my all or simply do nothing. Was I totally ready at this point? No. However, I knew I could no longer go on with the mask and with not doing ministry the way God designed. So here we go! With all the hurt and pain that I still felt, I decided to pull myself up piece by piece. After all, there are people who are depending on me. There are people who are assigned to my hands. There are souls waiting to hear me, and while I knew I could not neglect self-care, I knew I had to get it right with God! By the way, all of this did not happen overnight, as this was a span of months!

This was a process! So, I repented to the Lord and asked for forgiveness and restoration, and I asked Him to help me with this because I was done allowing grief to have me go through the motions.

GRIEVING

My Journey: Growing Through Grief

Grieving is a verb which means to distress mentally, or to cause to feel grief or sorrow. Everyone grieves differently, and I often say that you can't tell someone how to grieve or how long to grieve. For me, the initial process was delayed, or so I thought.

My personal grieving process was normal yet complex. I know that sounds like an oxymoron, but I am wired differently than most people. I kept going and tried to suppress the feelings that were there, and not only did this cause harm to myself but also to those around me. I did not take a break. I believe we buried my father on Saturday, and I preached the next Sunday. Yes, you heard correctly, I preached the next Sunday.

I never thought I would be affected this severely. I mean, I had both grandmothers to die, and although that hurt like crazy; this was on another level. While grief may be a process to me, I did not handle the entire process well. If I were to grade myself in certain areas, I would definitely not give myself a passing score. Some would say that I am being a bit too hard on myself, after all this was my father. However, I allowed it to pull me into mindsets and attitudes that I know were not pleasing to God.

Some say there are five stages of grief, while others say there are seven. Well, since I am not a mental health specialist, I will talk on the five. It is important to know that everyone will not experience each step in the grieving process, nor will they experience them in a certain order. The stages of the grieving process are something that I have never thought of. However, when I stopped and did personal reflection, I realized that I, too, went through different stages of the process.

STAGE 1: DENIAL

During this stage of the grieving process, a person denies the reality of what is happening. So, in turn, you do not live in actual reality, but you live in a reality that you prefer or make up. During this stage, you become numb to the process and feel emotions such as shock, disbelief, and fear. In the beginning, I did not believe I experienced actual denial but felt that I experienced many of the emotions that extend from it. However, in looking back, there were times I would call his cell phone after he died to see if he would answer. I remember on one of those occasions, my mother answered his phone, but I was at least hoping that it would go to voicemail so that I could hear his voice. In visiting my mother, I would go with the hopes that maybe, just maybe he would still be in the room. However, each time I was severely disappointed. From the very first text message, my sister sent saying that my dad thought he had cancer, fear and shock shook me to my very core. When he found out on Christmas Eve, December 24, 2014, that it was stage 4, I felt those emotions increase and intensify to levels I had never felt before. Now I realize it was even at the beginning that I walked in denial. I was thinking, "this is not happening; this cannot be happening; this is not real!" Then I recall my sister sending me another text saying that my father had passed out in Food Lion. Again I didn't want to believe that things were as bad as they were. So I attempted to rationalize it in my mind by saying, maybe he just needed to eat something, or he was tired. The truth is, I was in denial. I remember his doctor meeting with my sisters and me and telling us straight forward, "Your father is going to die!" At that moment, it was as if a jolt of electricity went through me. However, I still didn't believe him because there were times when in his sickness, where he would look better. So that meant hope, right?

However, once my denial started to subside, I began to feel every emotion that I tried to hide and suppress.

STAGE 2: ANGER

Typically, once the effects of denial wear off and you come back to reality, anger can set in. During this stage, one can and often will redirect the anger towards family and friends. In some cases, anger can even be directed at the one who is sick, dying, or has died; or even directed at God.

At this stage, I felt like the child holding his hand up in class, saying, "ME!" I was angry! First and foremost, I was angry with God. I know what you may be thinking, "you are a preacher/pastor, so how can you be angry with God. The short answer is "EASILY!" For one, being a pastor does not make me exempt from having human feelings and emotions. I think sometimes people tend to put us pastors on pedestals and raise us so high as to think we are immune to feelings and emotions. Many do not realize that the word anger appears over five hundred times in the Bible, and the only other emotion mentioned more is love. However, we are told in the Word to be angry but sin not, and I believe many times, the average person needs to see and hear what we go through as pastors as a testimony to help them. We cannot be so heavenly minded that we are no earthly good. I was angry with God because He did not heal my father. I fasted and interceded, I laid hands on him and prayed for him, and yet he still died. I began to wonder, "God, how could you let this happen?" I prayed and interceded for people before and watched God turn things around for them, therefore, surely I knew with everything that's within me that He would heal my father. However, He didn't, or did he?

Although I was hurt and broken, I still preached, and angry with God while doing it. I know that it can be too real for some of you, but it is the truth. I know what you are thinking, how could you do that. Well, the short answer is God gave me grace. He could have taken me down at any moment, but He did not, and I call that grace. I also internalized or suppressed my anger. I am the type of person to internalize my emotions, which I know can be dangerous. Yes, I do talk more today, but then I did not. Dr. Tim Clinton and Dr. Ron Hawkins say, "Sometimes people repress the anger, meaning they deny anger's presence. This is unhealthy because even though it may not be observable, the anger is still present—turned inward on the person. Repressed anger can lead to numerous emotional and physical problems, including depression, anxiety, hypertension, and ulcers. Or people may suppress their anger, meaning they acknowledge anger and then stuff it. With this approach to coping, they redirect anger-driven energy into unrelated activities. This can be effective, though it neglects to address the root causes of anger. One risk is that people who suppress may become cynical or passive-aggressive—an indirect form of revenge manifesting as sarcasm, lack of cooperation, gossip, and so on." This was me! I repressed, suppressed, and internalized my anger. Daily I would feel that at any moment, I could explode, and that was with the Holy Ghost. However, I thank Him for being a constrainer! I had intense anger towards my father's cancer doctor. I felt as if he built his and our hopes only to let us come crashing down. He told us that my father would be healed and that he was giving him the best and the strongest treatment, only to turn around a few months later, and we're burying him. I wanted to sue the doctor, and I wanted to fight the doctor. I wanted him to feel this hurt that I was now feeling. After all, he promised and didn't deliver!

My family felt the brunt of my anger, and I believe that it was because they were the closest. I would often be snappy with my wife and kids, and some days just downright rude and sarcastic. I honestly do not know how my wife put up with my attitude because some days were worse than others. My kids literally walked on eggshells around me, and that upset me even more. I think at that point; I was also angry with myself for putting them through this. After many days, possibly weeks walking around like this, my wife finally had enough. I finally heard that infamous, "Mike!" She said, "you need to get it together because we have not done anything to you for you to be acting like this." You know what? She was absolutely right, so I began to channel it back to the source where I was mad first, and that was God!

STAGE 3: BARGAINING

Bargaining is defined as negotiating the terms and conditions of a transaction. The feeling of guilt can come with bargaining. I did my fair share of bargaining with God through the entire process of my father's illness. I bargained with the hopes that the outcome and even the timing would change. I felt helpless and vulnerable and didn't know what to do; therefore, I did what I felt or what I now know was the natural thing to do. I would say, "God, if you heal my father, I promise I will serve you forever." I cannot tell you the number of times I asked this of God; however, instead of getting better, we watched his feeble body continue to deteriorate. Shortly after, the feeling of guilt came like a raging whirlwind. Questions began to run through my mind constantly: why didn't I see the signs (after all, he was losing weight and my mother would constantly hem uniforms)? What if he would have got medical attention sooner? What if we would have got a second opinion on his method of treatment (there were two hospitals in the city). I wanted life to be back as it was. I wanted to casually walk in my parent's home like I used to and at times grab my father from behind and tell him, "I got you now, what are you going to do?" I wanted him to come back to us, and we continue on life as normal. I wanted to have a "do-over" so that we could spot this sickness quicker and get treatment. I wanted a "do-over" because even as a grown man, I felt there was still so much more for me to learn from him. I wanted a "do-over" so I could apologize again for the things I did wrong. I wanted a "do-over" because I felt guilty that I did not care for him physically as much as my sisters did while he was sick. After all, they are the nurses, but I wanted to do more. Yes, I felt a pang of deep-seated guilt that I didn't do enough. Although we are a very close-knit family, I felt I should have told him that I loved him and that I appreciated him more, and I wanted God to heal him not on the other side but on this side!

STAGE 4: DEPRESSION

You will read that I do touch on the topic of depression in my chapter on Mental. However, here I will say that I had functional depression. I still worked, preached, and did things within the community. I still followed my daily routine. However, this also means that I wore the tears of a clown. For those of you who may not know what that means, well here it is. When you see clowns, you notice that they always have to put on a smiling face to entertain others. The tears of a clown describe someone who appears joyful and happy but inside is emotionally distraught. That was me! Outwardly I was still that charismatic Michael, however inwardly, it felt as if I was sinking in quicksand. Emptiness grew stronger and deeper than I thought it could. When God did not accept my bargaining agreement, it made me reflect on the loss, which caused me to have depression. My emotions were all over the place during this time. I would just cry and scream out of the blue, and there were times where I would even cuss up a storm. STOP IT!! DON'T JUDGE ME!! I CAN HEAR YOU! I would be by myself and would let them rip. I had the rawest emotions during this time. Every day I would listen to the Message I gave as I eulogized him. For me, I don't know if that was a good thing as it would send me back into uncontrollable crying and heaviness. There were major changes in my sleeping (as many nights, I found it hard to sleep) and my eating (as I turned to food). This was painful; it hurt, the isolation and loneliness were overwhelming. Although it may not have seemed like it, I began to withdraw from people so that I could deal with this alone. You do know that you can be surrounded by people and still be withdrawn and alone. I felt like I was regressing to a time when I was younger, where I would not let people in or allow them to get close. I thought that this would never end, and even today, during his birthday, Thanksgiving, Christmas, in March when he died, and at other valuable times throughout the years, I still have moments of sometimes intense heaviness.

STAGE 5: ACCEPTANCE

It took a while to get to this point. Now let's be clear, acceptance doesn't mean that I am ok with it, everything was not peachy keen, happy, uplifting, or had just blown over, but I have reached the point in which finally accepted that my father was gone and now there must be a new normal. No, I didn't like this reality, but I accepted it. Life as I knew it had been forever changed, and I had to make necessary adjustments. There was no more calling him for fixes around the house, no more calling him to look at or listen to the vehicles when something was wrong, and no more of his exquisite culinary creations. In other words, his good food! While I understand that not everyone reaches acceptance because they are not able to see past denial or anger, I am thankful that I have, although it was a process. As time went on, I would have more good days than bad though I think of regularly. To me, nothing or no one can replace him. However, through this process, I have learned again to not suppress my feelings and that I've had to grow and evolve. The truth is because of the way I was spiraling in the grieving process. I should have sought counseling. However, once again, I believed the lie of my black community that we do not need it, and the lie of how I would look like a pastor going to talk to someone. Although I did not seek counseling, I am thankful for a real support system that put up with me through the process. I finally accepted the truth that I had given so many others, and that was, he was healed on the other side.

TODAY

My Journey: Growing Through Grief

At the present moment, it has been six years since my father has been gone; however, I still miss him like it was yesterday. I don't know if I will ever get over the fact that he is gone, and I will not say each year is easier, but it's better than it was in the beginning. Each year, especially around the time of his death in March, I still feel the sadness of the occasion and often find myself getting a bit on edge. However, today I don't go over the edge, and have grown, and am more grounded than I was six years ago. Again, my feelings and emotions were running wild then, although I masked it well. I often tell people, do not let anyone tell you how long it should take you to get over a loved one. Feel what you feel but do not let those feelings cause you to do something regrettable. I almost did, I almost allowed my feelings to take me to a very dark place, but I thank God for every intervening moment.

So how did I make it through to this point? I am glad you asked! I came to the realization that grief really is synonymous with LOVE. Listen, I know it sounds strange, but the truth is people grieve the way they do because of their love for the deceased person. Therefore, when I came to the place of acceptance and any feelings thereafter, I realized that it's LOVE! That freed me to not feel the need to bottle my emotions or that I had to hold a certain demeanor because I am a man. This was love-driven. Not to mention a family friend sent me a private message telling me that I no longer have to be strong. When I received and read it, I don't know if words can express how freeing that was for me. I believe those were the words I was waiting for; someone to tell me to just let go!

I also began to pray and put the Word of God that I preached and ministered to others so often into practice in my own situation. I would pray the Scriptures back to God because when you belong to Him, you can hold Him to His Word. So it would be like, "Jesus, you said according to Your Word that You would not leave me comfortless (John 14:18). Jesus, You said in Your Word that Your grace is sufficient for me, and Your strength is made perfect in my weakness (2 Corinthians 12:9). Jesus, my soul is weary with sorrow, strengthen me according to your word (Psalm 119:28). Jesus, You said in Your Word you give strength to the weary, and you increase the power of the weak (Isaiah 40:29), and I need you to help me in and through this." So what I was doing was standing on the promises of God through prayer and His Word. Yes, the same God who I was mad at for not healing my father, was the same God to whom I was now praying and was the same God who stood waiting for me to come to Him to receive comfort, healing, deliverance, and to release the anger and hurt which I harbored inside.

Those who know me know that I am a worshipper at heart, and that is exactly what I did. I let my praise and worship fight through depression, anger, stress, and all other emotions which tried to keep me bound. Day in and day out, I would worship and sing praises to God until one day I finally felt something break over me. I had compiled a playlist and riding to and from work, I would have "Father Me" and "Praise Is What I Do" by Shekinah Glory, "I Will Rejoice" by Pastor William Murphy, and the one that truly helped me through that time was "Healing" by Richard Smallwood. Every day I would belt these songs from the rafters, worshipping and ushering myself into the very Presence of the Lord. We love to quote Psalm 16:11, "In thy presence is fulness of joy; at thy right hand there are pleasures forevermore." However, when you find yourself (as many of you have or will) in a situation as I was, you will realize the reality of the Word. I would constantly and consistently worship and worship and worship to gain strength from the Lord and to receive His joy. At other times I would talk to and motivate myself to take my life back. No, that's not a sign that you are crazy, as long as you don't answer yourself! Smile! However, I told myself, "Come on, Michael, remember who you are and LIVE"! That was a decision that I had to make that no one could make for me. I had to decide to heal, and that healing meant doing the internal and the external work. I had to apologize to my family and others, but that was part of doing the work. I repented to God for my actions towards Him and others, and every day I got up telling myself that I was going to make it.

I am thankful to have such a loving wife, who was my strength during that time. There were many nights where I would feel her hand placed in the center of my back, and she would be praying for me and would encourage me throughout the day. She is my real MVP; my Most Valuable Porscha! I also thank God for a great support team! Listen, my inner circle of support is like no other.

They allowed me (through the process) the opportunity to not be Pastor Mosley or Pastor Mike, but to just be Michael! Sometimes they would sit and say nothing and allow me to vent, to cry, and to throw tantrums, while at other times, they would pray for me, encourage me and let me know when I was out of pocket. Having that support team (at least for me) was vital and necessary. It is important to connect with or have people in your life that want to see you whole, healed, and healthy; and who will remind you that you are not the victim.

Today I am thankful. I am thankful for where I am in life and in mind because I have seen people not recover from a parent or loved one's death. Although my father did what he could to prepare us, I don't believe no one is ever fully prepared. However, I celebrate life today. Yes, I needed to mourn his passing. However, I realized that I couldn't do that to the point that I didn't celebrate his life, and I know from his talk that he wanted us to go on. The past is over, and the future hasn't happened yet. Therefore, as I go down memory lane and remember how happy he was seeing his grandchildren born, the joy he had from driving the school bus and training other bus drivers, how took time to build his man cave and plan horseshoe tournaments, and how as a grown man if I needed him he would be right there with no hesitation, and the way he gave my mother whatever she wanted; it gives me life to celebrate his life. I can also celebrate his life because, on his deathbed, I had the opportunity to lead him to Christ. HALLELUJAH! So, I am happy because I know where he is! That is part of what I do today to continue to grow past the feelings; I remember the good times.

I have learned and grown a lot from this experience. I have learned that it is ok to not be ok! Having emotions doesn't make me weak. They make me human. I came to the conclusion that admitting that I was not ok for me was the first step in letting go of the pain, and the way out of pain was to go through it. I have learned that as a man, you do not always have to be strong. We are taught as men that we must always have the "S" on our chest, we must be tough, and that we just need to "man up." However, being vulnerable does not make you any less of a man. As a matter of fact, everyone has moments of vulnerability, whether they admit it or not, and although vulnerability is scary, it can be powerful. I have learned that it is ok to have Christ and a counselor or therapist, because if I were to do it again, I would see one. This stigma for counselors or counseling for us black men must be removed and is an integral part of our healing. I have learned not to take the ones I love and who love me for granted and tell them you love them. That's why every day I embrace my wife and kids and show and tell them how much I love them. I have learned to nurture the ones that I love. Since life is finite, I have learned to live and enjoy life. I have learned that it is the simple things in life that can bring great joy. I have learned that I can't fix every problem and that really is ok. I have learned to laugh more and not take things so seriously.

The entire experience was a journey for me. When I think about a journey, I think of something that is long and strenuous. Journeys have the potential cost you energy, sweat, tears and even moments of wanting to give up and quit. What my journey did for me was it helped to develop a greater intestinal fortitude. Think about Olympic runners, especially long-distance; they must have the endurance to go on. My journey has given me the courage and endurance to continue even in the face of adversity.

My Journey: Growing Through Grief

One of the greatest things my journey did was it showed me myself! Within me there had to be a confrontation between the boy who was dependent upon and wanted to hold on to his father and the man who was now a husband and a father himself. You may have to wait for the next installment to see the details of that confrontation. In the midst of the pain, I was able to see the areas in the areas in my life that needed fixing, healing, and adjusting. Sometimes a thing has to be broken in order to heal and grow properly. All I am saying is that sometimes healing requires hurt. I would have never grown past and dealt with the issues of my heart if this journey had not taken place. One of the hardest things, yet one of the most freeing things I did was to turn the mirror on me and tell myself there is more growing that you have to do because you are not there yet. My journey has shown me the similarities between my father and me. Today, everyone tells me how much I look just like him. I am like him in more ways than I thought, and when he left us, I knew it was time for me to step up and assume the position of leading my family. We are not meant to walk through life and carry the heavyweight alone, although sometimes you can be in or with a crowd of people and still feel alone. Each of us is on our own unique journey through life. The journey is filled with ups, downs, highs, and lows; from all which we are to learn valuable lessons. My prayer is that in my journey through pain and grief that you saw me, not the Pastor, not the preacher, (although I could not help but to put some scripture in), but Michael. This has been part of My Journey! Although I didn't tell it ALL (as it would have been too long), it is my hope that my journey would inspire you to keep pushing through tough and depressing times, because they will come.

My Journey Devotional

CONFRONT IT!

As the Philistine moved closer to attack him, David ran quickly toward the battle line to meet him. 1 Samuel 17:48 (NIV)

There are times in our lives when we are faced with giants. These are things, situations and circumstances that may seem insurmountable and undefeatable. It could be grief, failures of the past, sickness, worry, fear, debt etc. David was faced with a giant that threatened the nation. However instead of running from it, he ran towards it to face it. Though he may have seemed weak to the giant, he had confidence that he would be victorious because he was not facing it in his own strength.

What giant(s) do you need to confront today?

_____

_____

_____

_____

_____

_____

_____

_____

_____

What or whom is keeping you from confronting your giant(s) today?

_____

_____

_____

_____

_____

_____

_____

_____

My Journey: Growing Through Grief

Put together your personal strategy or plan to confront your giant:

_____

_____

_____

_____

_____

_____

_____

_____

DON'T' SUPRESS IT, FEEL IT!

There is a time for everything, and a season for every activity under the heavens: a time to be born and a time to die, a time to plant and a time to uproot, a time to kill and a time to heal, a time to tear down and a time to build, a time to weep and a time to laugh, a time to mourn and a time to dance… Ecclesiastes 3:1-4

Solomon allows us to know that there is a time for everything and a season for every activity under the heavens. Although these times and seasons for us can be largely unknowable, we must realize that they are still in God's perfect timing. Feeling different emotions that come with grief, hurt, betrayal or loss (on any level) are natural and meant to be experienced because we're human. None of what we feel when we are going through is wrong or means that we are faithless, it means that it's just your time.

What is the greatest pain(s) you have experienced or are currently experiencing?

_____

_____

_____

_____

_____

_____

_____

_____

_____

Dig deep and describe the emotions or feelings that went along with each pain. Search internally for those you have suppressed.

_____

_____

_____

_____

_____

_____

_____

_____

How did those feelings affect you? Put together your

personal strategy or plan to deal with those

feelings: Remember having them is not bad, it means you

are human.

_____

_____

_____

_____

_____

_____

_____

_____

WE NEED EACH OTHER!

If either of them falls down, one can help the other up. But pity anyone who falls and has no one to help them up. Ecclesiastes 4:10

We were never created to walk this life alone. We were created to help and lift each other in tumultuous times. While it is a blessing to give help, it is also a blessing to receive it. This is why Solomon tells us that two are better than one, because companionship and friendship has its benefits. It's important to accept the listening ear and the helping hand of people around you who sincerely want to help. Paul said, "No temptation has overtaken you except what is common to mankind." Our situation is not unique! Other men and women have faced similar experiences and have overcome. Therefore, we need the help of others to move beyond our pain.

In your experiences past or present, what keeps you from seeking or receiving help?

_____

_____

_____

_____

_____

_____

_____

_____

What would make you open to receiving help?

_____

_____

_____

_____

_____

_____

_____

_____

What do you look for in help from people and what is your reaction when the help doesn't look as you expected?

_____

_____

_____

_____

_____

_____

_____

_____

KNOW THAT GOD IS NEAR!

He heals the brokenhearted and binds up their wounds. Psalm 147:3

Some say that hurting times will show you what you are made of, however I believe these times show you what God is made of. The writer of Psalm 147:3 allows us to know that God cares for each of us. It is amazing to know that our God is not distant but close enough that he is aware and heals our broken hearts and wounds, and he is sympathetic enough to want us healed. He does not just heal the outward, but he also heals the deep emotional scars that we hide, suppress or carry inward. Psalm 34:18 tells us, The LORD is close to the brokenhearted and saves those who are crushed in spirit. When we are in places of grief, sadness, fear, anger etc., and are in need of something greater than ourselves, God would have us to know that not only is His Presence with us when life is hard but He is near!

My Journey: Growing Through Grief

In the tough times of life, have you ever felt God wasn't near? Explain a situation and your feelings:

_____

_____

_____

_____

_____

_____

_____

_____

Knowing that God is near, is it still hard to fully trust Him or lean on Him first in tough times? Why or Why not?

_____

_____

_____

_____

_____

_____

_____

_____

What does Psalm 34:18 and Psalm 147:3 mean to you?
How will you apply them in hard times?

_____

_____

_____

_____

_____

_____

_____

_____

_____

POUR IT ON HIM!

Trust in him at all times, you people; **pour out your hearts to him***, for God is our refuge.*

Psalm 62:8 (NIV)

What do you do with feelings of grief, pain, hurt, disappointment, and sorrow etc.? Whatever you're feeling at whatever moment, God invites his people to pour out our sorrow, disappointments, hurt, pain, grief and even joy to him. He already knows the trials and the troubles and we face, but his desire is for us to come to Him and talk to Him about them. He wants us to come and say, "God help me! God I'm hurting and I'm grieving! HELP!" Cast all your anxiety on him because he cares for you (1 Peter 5:7). Today whatever you are facing throw it away from you and place it onto God.

In what areas have I not trusted God fully?

_____

_____

_____

_____

_____

_____

_____

_____

What confidence do you have in God that you can pour out your heart to Him?

_____

_____

_____

_____

_____

_____

_____

_____

Let's Pray

Heavenly Father, I come thanking you that you hear me. Today I pour every anxiety, worry, disappointment, hurt and pain on you because I trust that you can heal me in every area of brokenness. I don't submit to my circumstances, but I submit my feelings to you, the One who controls the circumstances. In Jesus Name. Amen.